D1528891

SUPER CUTE!

Baby
Foxes

by Megan Borgert-Spaniol

BELLWETHER MEDIA • MINNEAPOLIS, MN

Note to Librarians, Teachers, and Parents:

Blastoff! Readers are carefully developed by literacy experts and combine standards-based content with developmentally appropriate text.

Level 1 provides the most support through repetition of high-frequency words, light text, predictable sentence patterns, and strong visual support.

Level 2 offers early readers a bit more challenge through varied simple sentences, increased text load, and less repetition of high-frequency words.

Level 3 advances early-fluent readers toward fluency through increased text and concept load, less reliance on visuals, longer sentences, and more literary language.

Level 4 builds reading stamina by providing more text per page, increased use of punctuation, greater variation in sentence patterns, and increasingly challenging vocabulary.

Level 5 encourages children to move from "learning to read" to "reading to learn" by providing even more text, varied writing styles, and less familiar topics.

Whichever book is right for your reader, Blastoff! Readers are the perfect books to build confidence and encourage a love of reading that will last a lifetime!

This edition first published in 2016 by Bellwether Media, Inc.

No part of this publication may be reproduced in whole or in part without written permission of the publisher. For information regarding permission, write to Bellwether Media, Inc., Attention: Permissions Department, 5357 Penn Avenue South, Minneapolis, MN 55419.

Library of Congress Cataloging-in-Publication Data

Borgert-Spaniol, Megan, 1989- author.
 Baby Foxes / by Megan Borgert-Spaniol.
   pages cm. – (Blastoff! Readers. Super Cute!)
 Summary: "Developed by literacy experts for students in kindergarten through grade three, this book introduces baby foxes to young readers through leveled text and related photos"– Provided by publisher.
 Audience: Ages 5-8
 Audience: K to grade 3
 Includes bibliographical references and index.
 ISBN 978-1-62617-215-9 (hardcover: alk. paper)
 1. Foxes–Infancy–Juvenile literature. I. Title. II. Series: Blastoff! Readers. 1, Super Cute!
 QL737.C22B6185 2016
 599.775'139–dc23

2015009731

Printed in the United States of America, North Mankato, MN.

Table of Contents

Fox Pups!

Baby foxes are called pups. They are born in a **den**.

Most pups have brothers and sisters. Some **litters** have more than 10 pups.

Newborn pups stay close to mom. She keeps them warm and fed.

Dad helps mom protect the pups. **Predators** will try to eat them.

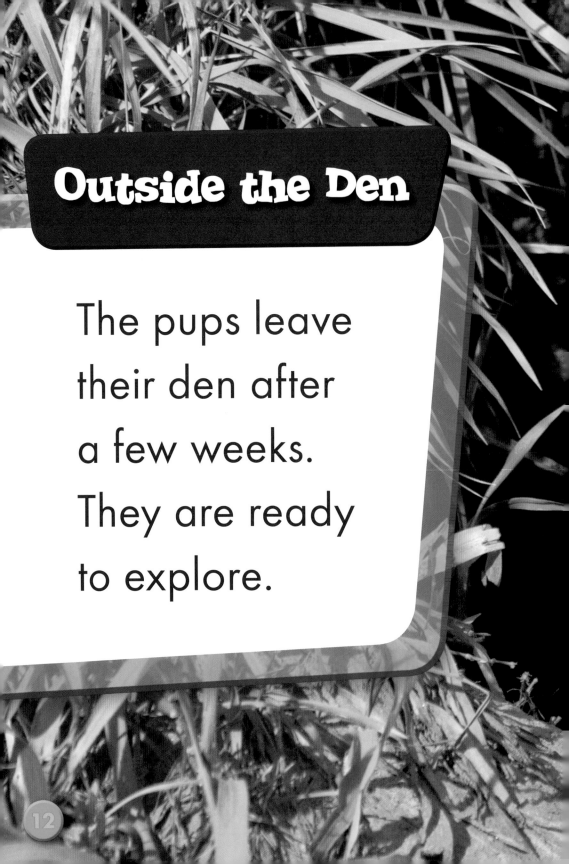

Outside the Den

The pups leave their den after a few weeks. They are ready to explore.

They like to
play together.
They **wrestle**
and **pounce**.

Mom and dad start to bring meat for dinner. The pups also still **nurse**.

Time to Hunt

Soon the pups learn to hunt. They **stalk** one another to practice.

Their parents bring them **prey** to catch. Go for it, pup!

Glossary

den—a place where animals stay safe; foxes build dens in the sides of hills, under rocks, and inside logs.

litters—groups of babies that are born together

newborn—just recently born

nurse—to drink mom's milk

pounce—to leap on top of something

predators—animals that hunt other animals for food

prey—animals that are hunted by other animals for food

stalk—to secretly follow

wrestle—to fight in a playful way

To Learn More

AT THE LIBRARY
Gardener, Jane P. *Fennec Foxes*. New York, N.Y.: Bearport Publishing, 2014.

Green, Emily. *Foxes*. Minneapolis, Minn.: Bellwether Media, 2011.

Lindgren, Astrid. *The Tomten and the Fox*. New York, N.Y.: Putnam & Grosset Group, 1997.

ON THE WEB
Learning more about foxes is as easy as 1, 2, 3.

1. Go to www.factsurfer.com.

2. Enter "foxes" into the search box.

3. Click the "Surf" button and you will see a list of related web sites.

With factsurfer.com, finding more information is just a click away.

Index

The images in this book are reproduced through the courtesy of: Gerard Lacz/ Age Fotostock/ Superstock,
front cover, pp. 4-5; Reinhard Holzl/ ImageBroker/ Superstock, pp. 6-7; Geoffrey Kuchera, pp. 8-9;
Roberta Olenick/ Glow Images, pp. 10-11; Sokolov Alexey, pp. 12-13; Juniors Bildarchiv/ Age Fotostock,
pp. 14-15; Jasper Doest/ Corbis, pp. 16-17; Menno Schaefer, pp. 18-19; NHPA/ Superstock, pp. 20-21.